Praise for Being a Proverbial Student

"There can be a stark difference between getting a college degree and gaining a college education that fosters lifelong learning and servant leadership. Here in this succinct, insightful, and timely work, students and teachers alike will find ready help in the arts of genuine learning and authentic teaching as well as living the well-examined life of Christian faithfulness. *Tolle lege!* Take up and read!"

— Dr. Robert A. Bryant,
Kristen Herrington Professor of
Religion Director, Cornelson Institute
for Christian Practice and Vocation
Department of Religion and
Philosophy Presbyterian College

"Anyone with an interest in higher education will find Dr. Jerry Williams's book a hidden treasure. He offers a healthy critique of a college education today which often sees its primary task as preparing students to earn a diploma and find a job. In contrast, he celebrates the deeper tasks of seeking knowledge and searching for wisdom.

As an academic, he offers his thoughts on a system which focuses on degrees and job preparation. He believes a more enlightened grounding for a university education is a focus on seeking wisdom and knowledge. While his book is written for college students, pastors, parents, and professors will also find it enlightening.

Dr. Williams is a devout Christian and his writing reflects his convictions. I found his use of illustrative material from his personal life to be especially helpful. I wish I could have had him as a professor."

— Dr. Thomas W. Shane, D.Div.

"Overall I found the book very clear and practical in nature. … I really like the directness for each chapter and the questions that are posed to the reader about the 2 ways that attending a college can be looked at. … illustrations [are] very helpful and clear. Bottom line: I would purchase this book and give it to every student going to college in my church."

— Richard Carroll,
Pastor of Discipleship
Emerald Bible Fellowship,
Eugene, Oregon

"I used [a preliminary version of] *Being a Proverbial Student* for two years in our First Year Integration course. It added a key missing dimension to the course. With very few students attending a Christian college, understanding the lessons presented by Dr. Williams is essential. I highly recommend this book."

— Dr. Gary W. Ewen,
Dean of the School of Business and
Leadership, Professor of Management
and Leadership Studies
Colorado Christian University

BEING A PROVERBIAL STUDENT

GETTING A DEGREE GETTING AN EDUCATION

by
JERAL R. WILLIAMS

Being a Proverbial Student: Getting a Degree vs. Getting an Education
Copyright © 2018 by Jeral R. Williams
Published by Deep River Books
Sisters, Oregon
www.deepriverbooks.com

All rights reserved. No part of this book may be reproduced or transmitted in any form or by any means, electronic or mechanical, including photocopying and recording, or by any information storage and retrieval system, without permission in writing from the publisher.

Unless otherwise noted, Scriptures are taken from the *Revised Standard Version of the Bible*, copyright © 1946, 1952, and 1971 the Division of Christian Education of the National Council of the Churches of Christ in the United States of America. Used by permission. All rights reserved.

Scriptures marked PHILLIPS are taken from *The New Testament in Modern English* by J. B. Phillips, copyright © 1960, 1972 J. B. Phillips. Administered by The Archbishops' Council of the Church of England. Used by permission.

ISBN–13: 9781632694744
LOC: 2018909857

Cover Design by Jason Enterline

Printed in the USA
2018—First Edition
27 26 25 24 23 22 21 20 19 18   10 9 8 7 6 5 4 3 2 1

Caroline
Be A life-long learner

To Jeny (my wife), and Scott, Dawn,
and Shane (our children).

Table of Contents

Acknowledgments 9

Introduction. 11

Chapter 1   Being a Proverbial Student 15

Chapter 2   Gittin' a Degree 19

Chapter 3   Remolding is What God Desires 25

Chapter 4   Be Curious about Ideas. 33

Chapter 5   Context 37

Chapter 6   Where There's a Will 55

Chapter 7   Decision-Making 65

Chapter 8   An Attitude 71

Chapter 9   Spiritual Wisdom and Academic Wisdom 77

Chapter 10   Graduation and Commencement. 83

Chapter 11   A Lifelong Proverbial Student. 85

List of Proverbs. 93

Endnotes 95

Acknowledgments

Over the years, I have expressed many different ideas in lectures, and enjoyed thousands of conversations about those ideas with students and colleagues. I have observed first-hand how they can contribute to intellectual growth in students, both Christian and non-Christian. I acknowledge the contributions of many people to those ideas. I thank Carl Simmons and the staff at Deep River Books for their contributions to, and support for, this endeavor. During the editing process I suffered a serious stroke. Their patience and support during my recovery is deeply appreciated.

My students are too numerous to mention and many of the conversations long forgotten, but I thank them for helping me grow as a thinking person and for the development of the ideas you find in this book.

My colleagues are many and our discussions (often arguments) numerous. I thank them.

My mentors are fewer, but nonetheless very valuable for my growth. I thank them.

Many Christians to whom my wife and I opened our homes and our lives have contributed in big and small ways to my personal development and to this book. I thank them.

I thank my family for their love and continued contributions to my life. Only God comes before my family in what I truly value.

Jeral (Jerry) Williams
Mobile, Alabama
2018

Introduction

According to the Gospels, after Christ's baptism he spent time in the wilderness, where He faced a time of temptation. For Christian students, college is often a time in the wilderness and a time of great temptations. If they go away to school, support systems found in their homes, families, schools, and churches are behind them. The separation can create a vast wilderness with many temptations.

University life is also a time of great opportunity. The formation of new friendships, the discovery of boundaries, the growth of self-reliance, and other situations are great opportunities for spiritual growth. Students who overcome temptations, learn from mistakes, and learn to depend on God are strengthened by their wilderness experiences.

This combination of temptations and opportunities weaves a large, complex tapestry of experiences. Successes and failures, joys and repentance, move quickly and repeatedly in and out of the average student's life.

I know firsthand the complex nature of a Christian student's life on a university campus. During my forty-five years in higher education, my wife and I had strong personal relationships with students from a wide variety of home, community, cultural, financial, and church backgrounds. We lived in community with Christian students; we regularly led nondenominational fellowship groups and denominational church groups. Some students were barely beginning their faith walks, while others were well into their relationships with Christ. Whatever their background, one dynamic remained true—the ebb and flow of triumphs and trials in their Christian journeys were continuous.

We shared many joys with them. We also shared disappointments when students stumbled, but stood beside them as they fought to recover. We grieved with them when they lost friends, family, first loves, and career opportunities. At the same time, we celebrated when they gained new insights, formed new friendships, and deepened their relationships with God. We sang, prayed, and shared a host of other meaningful experiences with Christian students. We loved them and were loved by them.

As a result, I clearly understand why the most frequent advice parents, pastors, campus leaders, and other advisors give to Christian students is focused on Christian living. Very good books are written, excellent sermons are preached, small group discussions are led, counseling sessions are held, and Bible studies are conducted—all centered on Christian *survival*. Facing sexual temptation, resisting drugs and alcohol abuse, forming and losing relationships, overcoming bad roommates, bad cafeteria food, even coping with "liberal" professors are but a few of the many topics frequently addressed.

Survival issues are obviously very important. Students need to prepare to face temptations. They need warnings. They need to feel support in the wilderness. They need to hear how others have survived. They need to know forgiveness and redemption.

Another critical part of a Christian student's campus experiences, not stressed as often as Christian living, is the academic experience of a Christian student. What does it mean to be a Christian student? How should a Christian student approach academic activities?

I believe academic issues are very important, and yet they are vastly underrepresented in the literature and messages of pastors, parents, and others ministering to college students. The academic advice given to many Christian students is superficial—"Christ wants you to do your best, so study hard." While the statement is true, it does not begin to address the deeper academic issues confronting Christian students. Suggestions about specific academic issues are often limited to warnings about wrong or bad ideas students may encounter from the teachings of non-Christian professors.

I believe God has deeper, more positive, academic advice for students. I believe God wants Christian students to be "Proverbial" students. A Proverbial student attends college in the pursuit of knowledge—and a university education provides the foundation for a lifelong quest for knowledge, understanding, and wisdom.

The United Negro College Fund has a meaningful motto: "A mind is a terrible thing to waste." Anyone with a healthy mind has the responsibility to see that it is not wasted. That responsibility is a deep one for a Christian.

I believe that being a Proverbial student is a Christian responsibility. I believe a wasted mind is not pleasing to God. Proverbial students should lead examined lives. Proverbial students should gain knowledge and understanding. Proverbial students should become wise. I pray God grants all Christian students the wisdom to accept the challenge.

I have written this book to encourage Christian students to be Proverbial students. I also hope that parents and advisors of Christian students, and anyone who enjoys an examined life, will read this message and mentor students accordingly.

Chapter 1

Being a Proverbial Student

"An intelligent mind acquires knowledge, and the
ear of the wise seeks knowledge"

(Prov. 18:15).

In order to understand what it means to be a Proverbial student, consider the difference between earning a degree and gaining an education. The correct choice for a Christian is clear, under the authority of the Bible.

Take a Bible and skim the book of Proverbs. The verses do not need to be closely studied, just quickly scanned; in other words, read Proverbs as if you were quickly reading a newspaper.

When you're finished, address the following questions:

Do the writers of Proverbs offer advice about individual test scores?

Do the writers of Proverbs offer advice about grades?

Do the writers of Proverbs offer advice about easy courses?

Do the writers of Proverbs offer advice about course times?

Do the writers of Proverbs offer advice about easy teachers?

Do the writers of Proverbs offer advice about majors?

Do the writers of Proverbs offer advice about career choices?

or

Do the writers indicate that knowledge, understanding, and wisdom are important?

Even a cursory scan reveals that the obvious and very strong stress in Proverbs is on knowledge, understanding, and wisdom. While many proverbs apply to Christian living (including career ethics), the primary appeal is to seek knowledge, understanding, and wisdom. And although knowledge, understanding, and wisdom are gained in a variety of ways and applied to many topics, I firmly believe the admonitions in Proverbs clearly apply to academic studies.

In my experience, students seeking *degrees* are interested in test scores, grades, ten o'clock classes, easy teachers, easy courses, majors, jobs, and careers. Students interested in an *education* seek knowledge, understanding, and wisdom. A Proverbial student knows the difference and chooses to pursue an education.

Clearly the Bible emphasizes education. Much of the content of one entire book of the Bible is concerned with knowledge, understanding, and wisdom. Christian advisors to college students give far more attention to far less emphasized parts of Scripture.

Be truthful: Are you going to college with knowledge, understanding, and wisdom as your primary focus? If the answer is yes, you are on the way to gaining an education—and to becoming a Proverbial student. I hope to encourage and deepen that process.

If no, then you are probably seeking a degree, and are probably more interested in test scores, grades, easy courses, good times, easy grades, majors, jobs, and careers. I hope to convince you of the importance of gaining knowledge, understanding, and eventually wisdom. I hope to convince you to be a Proverbial student.

In all of my classes, I taught students that the primary reason universities exist is knowledge. The faculty increase knowledge by performing research. Teachers dispense knowledge to students. Members of the university community provide knowledge to the general public. Since universities exist for knowledge, the primary academic interest for all students should be gaining knowledge. In my experience, this has not been the case.

In my opening lecture for every class, I asked students: "How many of you are interested in gaining knowledge?" Most students raised their hands, nodded, or in some way indicated an interest.

However, most students were taken aback when I pointed out that gaining knowledge meant that every day, when they came to class, I should be addressing something they did not know. I made the point that in order to gain knowledge, the lectures I would be giving, and books they would be reading, should be about information they did not already possess. If they already knew the ideas, they were not gaining anything. Clearly my hope was that every day they would walk out of class thinking: "I never heard that before!"

The majority (not all) of students realized that they were not really interested in gaining knowledge. In truth, they wanted to be entertained with information they already knew, and to get a grade for listening. The challenge to you is: Are you going to school to *gain* knowledge?

In my experience, most students, even Christian students, do not understand or appreciate an education. Even for those who understand an education, it is usually not their first priority for attending college.

My burden for Christian students runs deep. We live in a world that does not put a high value on wisdom, understanding, and knowledge. Social information, music, gossip, and material knowledge dominate radio, TV, the Internet and many other sources of communication. We need Christians to be leaders in holding knowledge, understanding, and wisdom in high regard.

My appeal is for you to be interested in gaining knowledge, understanding, and wisdom. I encourage you to be a Proverbial student.

Chapter 2

"Gittin' a Degree"

"A degree may be something to fall back on, but an education will lift you up"

(personal proverb).

I emphasize the distinction between getting a degree and gaining an education because understanding this distinction is critical for establishing the importance of being a Proverbial student. College athletics provides an excellent format for seeing this distinction.

You may love athletics. You may hate athletics. In either case, when you go to college you will find that athletics is an important part of campus life (on most university campuses). Even if certain aspects of sports seem repugnant, the prominent presence of sports on most university campuses is undeniable.

I love sports. I have been around college athletics for many years, in many capacities. I was an athlete (long ago and far away); I have been a coach, avid fan, administrator, and currently I help young athletes as a sports psychology consultant. Still, my love for college athletics does not blind me. I observe many serious problems with the "student" aspect of the student-athlete.

However, student problems are not unique to student-athletes. Because all students are influenced by the same cultural forces, academic problems for athletes are public manifestations of the same problems for all students. Athletes' academic problems are simply more obvious because they are much more in the public eye.

College athletics is a powerful reflection of the face of our society, a clear reflection of the values of our culture. By looking in that reflection, we can clearly see the emphasis on getting a degree and the lack of emphasis on earning an education. Understanding that reflection will help you further your understanding of the differences between getting a degree and gaining an education.

I want to make the distinction clearer by using a tongue-in-cheek interview of a college athlete:

TV Commentator: "Why are you staying in school?"

Athlete: "I'm stayin' in school to git my degree, to have somethin' to fall back on, in case I doesn't make it at the next level."

My tongue-in-cheek interview may be exaggerated, and the bad grammar and poor pronunciation a little overdramatic, but I know from many painful experiences that my fictional interview reflects a reality. Notice that there were no references to gaining an education, knowledge, understanding, or wisdom. Those concepts are foreign to most athletes—not all, but many.

Most athletes attend class to stay eligible. I frequently talk with individual athletes, as well as with groups. One of my favorite questions is: "Are you here to get a paid education, and all you have to do is play a sport you love? Or are you going to class just to stay eligible?" A very strong imagination is not necessary to know the preponderance of the responses I receive. Many do not even understand the question. Many understand, but think it is a silly question. Most who understand, and are honest, reply that they go to classes to stay eligible. Some partially understand the question and respond, "I am getting a degree paid for, and all I have to do is play a sport I love." Very, very few fully understand the question and respond that they are gaining an education.

When athletes realize that the dream of a pro career is over, many try to get a degree in the hopes that this piece of paper will get them a job. Unfortunately, the piece of paper has great value only if they have the knowledge it represents. Very few pursue an education and gain knowledge or understanding. Most are interested in eligibility, and at best, interested in degrees.

These attitudes about degrees and education are shaped by society; in the case of athletes, the media, fans, and coaches play a big role. Although many of the media have degrees, most do not have an education. Although many fans have degrees, many do not. Coaches have degrees, but few have an education. The predominant tendency is to believe that athletes go to college to stay eligible and, if possible, get a degree. Courses are taken to stay eligible, not to gain an education.

On television, radio, and the Internet, the bias is clearly demonstrated by broadcasters and fans in several ways. I commonly hear broadcasters and commentators opine that a student should turn pro as soon as possible. They say such blather as, "You only go to school to get a job—and if you have a job that will make you a millionaire, you should take it."

Unfortunately, I have only to look at several major sports stars from my current hometown to see the harm of this prevailing attitude. The particular young men I have in mind will go nameless for obvious reasons. They went to college and did not get an education; they went for athletics and attended class to stay eligible. They were high draft choices in their respective sports. They *were* millionaires. They are now bankrupt, both financially and morally. They are a drain on their communities and society. Their stories are all too common. Without an education, they have no way to contribute after their brief careers are over.

A few years ago, I spoke at a meeting of potential high-draft choices in several sports. I told them that the first rule of common-sense economics is to always spend less money than you make. Good knowledge and a wise practice. One particular player was there who I liked personally, but I also knew him well enough to know that he was a train wreck waiting to happen. He looked at me like I was crazy. As soon as he got his signing bonus he overspent the amount on a car, stereo system, and other material items. Since that time he has been bankrupt, and even spent time in prison. He even had a degree, but not even the first level of economic knowledge, understanding, and wisdom.

Degrees are important; someone with a degree has a better chance of surviving and contributing to society than someone without a degree. However, those few athletes who pursue an education have a far greater chance of contributing to our society.

It is important to note that I do not believe athletes are any more degree-oriented than other students—as I said, athletics provides a reflection of our society. The academic problems of athletes are reflections of the problems of all students, including Christian students. Knowledge, understanding, and wisdom are not high on the priority list for degree-seekers.

Obviously, with the exception of Christian athletes, Christian students do not have to stay eligible to participate in a sport. However, they have a strong eligibility desire: They desire to be eligible for a degree. In order to stay eligible, Christian students are just as prone as athletes to select certain teachers, select easier classes, have convenient time schedules, and attend classes and take tests merely to stay eligible to get a degree. Knowledge, understanding, and wisdom are not high priorities.

I would like the culture to change. I dream of the time I hear an athlete respond to the media by saying, "I am staying in school to gain an education. If I am privileged enough to become a professional athlete, I will earn a lot of money. I want to have knowledge of economics, of people, of history, of the arts, of politics, and other fundamental areas of knowledge, and to use that knowledge and the money to positively influence my culture."

I have a similar dream for you. If you see your primary purpose in college as gaining knowledge, then you will enroll in courses to gain knowledge of economics, of people, of history, of the arts, of politics, and other fundamental areas, rather than just trying to stay eligible for a degree. The time and ease of the teacher will not factor into your decision. You will discuss knowledge with peers and faculty. You will go over exams trying to understand the material you did not understand, rather than just trying to get a better score. You will attend public lectures and performances because you want the knowledge and experience, rather than because they are assigned. You will see assignments as opportunities to learn, rather than as hurdles to jump for a degree.

When you pursue an education, a degree is a byproduct of that education. Degrees are important when they represent knowledge gained. A degree without knowledge is a sham. Too often, degrees are not an indication of knowledge gained, but rather courses passed.

I clearly understand many of the problems shaped by our culture, and reflected by the problems in athletes and other students, are spiritual. Education alone will not solve all of the issues. However, an education will increase knowledge. From knowledge, with the help of the Holy Spirit, comes understanding and wisdom. Gaining knowledge, understanding, and wisdom will increase a Christian's ability to be a positive influence in our world. God's love, joy, and peace are desperately needed in our ever-increasingly complex world. An education will help you be God's servant, face the complexities, and better impact our very needy world.

Chapter 3

Remolding Is What God Desires

"The fear of the Lord is the beginning of knowledge;
fools despise wisdom and instruction"

(Prov. 1:7).

I love Romans 12:2 in the Phillips translation of the Bible: "Don't let the world around you squeeze you into its own mold, but let God remake you so that your whole attitude of mind is changed." I believe the world is clearly and strongly squeezing students into the "degree achievement" or "go to college to get a job" mold as the primary (if not sole) reason to attend college.

I understand the world's mold for students, because it shaped my own entry into higher education. I went to college because earning a degree was expected of me. I took tests to get good grades. I did well on tests because I was a very competitive person. Clearly, as a young man, I was not a Proverbial student.

My father was too poor to attend college until after World War II. The GI Bill enabled him, in his thirties, to enter Kansas State University. He was bright, motivated, and a man of great character. Through hard work, he earned a degree. The degree led to economic success for him and our family (after I left home, of course!). He and my mother wanted the same for their sons. My brother and I were raised with the clear expectation that we would go to college. My parents lived frugally and gave up a lot to enable that dream to come true.

Implicit in those expectations was the understanding that I would go to college to earn a degree, which would enable me to have a good job and have a successful career. As a young man, I never understood any other reason to go to college. My parents molded me in this way because that was the mold that would make a huge difference in the life of our family.

Please be very clear: My parents were wonderful people, and I am not being critical of them. The mold of my parents is not a bad mold. A degree/career mold is far more beneficial than many other molds. But what I am presenting in this book is an even better mold for going to college—one I hope you will understand and adopt.

Somehow, somewhere along my journey, I learned this higher and better reason to attend college—to gain knowledge and pursue an education. Good grades, degrees, jobs, and a career are not bad; however, they should be *byproducts, not the goals*, for attending college. Within me, the world's mold was remolded by God into an interest in knowledge and an education.

Unfortunately, in my teaching experience, most of my Christian students were squeezed into a degree/career mold as readily as other students. They needed to be remolded.

Even students with high academic abilities and expectations were just as squeezed as other students. They often failed to pursue an education. They avoided challenging courses because good grades are needed to get into medical school or other professional schools. They minimized courses that would educate them because they were solely focused on their careers.

They failed to understand that medical school would teach them medicine; law school would teach them law; pharmacy school would teach them pharmacy; dental school would teach them dentistry. They failed to see the need for a broad base of knowledge; they failed to become educated people. They needed to be remolded.

I have a friend who has major responsibilities for admissions to a medical school; he bemoans the lack of an undergraduate education in many of the applicants. He believes educated students not only have a better chance of getting into medical school but will have more productive careers. His concern has two points.

First, the medical school will teach students medicine. Courses of study that try to teach medical knowledge at the undergraduate level, in the hopes of increasing the chances of getting into medical school, are probably a waste of a student's time. Students seeking admission will have better interviews with admission counselors if they have a broad education, in addition to the science information needed to have a good score on the MEDCAT exam.

His second point is that surveys of medical school graduates provide strong evidence for a focus on education. The first few years out of medical school, doctors report a need for more medical knowledge. The next few years, they report the need to better understand economics. Then as they become influential in the community, they wish they had a better understanding of the arts, politics, world geography, history, and many other academic areas.

Too many students do not understand the importance of an education. They have no need for the electives that they believe get in the way of their career. Students fail to understand that in addition to high grade point averages and good scores on standardized tests, the best professional schools want well-educated students.

My point is underscored by a conversation I overheard in my favorite sushi bar. A student was bemoaning the fact that she had specialized in a quasi-medical undergraduate curriculum in the hopes of increasing her chances of getting into medical school. She had failed. She was upset about not getting into medical school, but was even more disturbed and very perplexed about a friend who got into medical school. Her friend majored in English. She simply could not understand how a student majoring in English could get into medical school, when she had taken the quasi-medical curriculum and did not get in. It never occurred to her that the English major was in the education mold: She was better educated, had gained knowledge which enabled her to have a good score on the standardized exam, and enabled her to have a good interview.

Another example of the benefits of an education comes from the engineering field. When I was in academic administration, the engineering accreditation group faced a problem: Their research clearly showed that engineering students were making more money than liberal arts students when they first graduated from college, but that later in their careers the liberal arts students were making more than the engineers. They discovered that when engineers graduated, they had specific skills that made them more employable at that time. However, too often, engineers were expected to perform those skills throughout their entire careers. They got stuck in a niche. Students with communication and problem-solving skills were going higher in the companies, and eventually were the bosses of the engineers. The accrediting agency worked hard to change the mold of the engineering curriculum, to include courses that would give students communication skills, people skills, and other knowledge that would give them an education beyond a particular engineering skill.

The benefits of being a student with an education often occur in subtle ways. One of my eldest son's best friends graduated with honors as an electrical engineer. He was a very bright young man and landed an excellent job with educated colleagues from all around the United States who had attended the very best colleges.

He talked with me about the pressure he felt during coffee breaks early in his career. He was tested repeatedly to see if he could speak "proper English" (he was from the South), to see if he read good books, to see if he had any knowledge of politics, etc. He gained an understanding of how an education played a major role in how others viewed him and the role it could play in promotions, confidence to perform a task, and other job-related activities. He was a Proverbial student. He was curious about knowledge; he sought understanding beyond the information he needed to be an engineer. He had a very successful career.

Another example is a very good student who was my advisee. He was a psychology major, and late in his junior year he decided he wanted to be an architect. He was thinking of changing his major, possibly to engineering. I suggested that he go to an architectural school and see what they advised him.

He took my advice, and when he got back from his interview he came in my office with a sly smile. He was advised to stay in psychology. The architectural advisors told him they would teach him architecture. They would teach him about materials, plans, and all that went into being an architect. They needed people who could integrate plans with the behavior of the people who would be using the buildings and other spaces. They believed the knowledge of psychology would make him a better architect. Once again knowledge, not a particular major, would enable him to have a good future. He was accepted into a very competitive school and went on to become an architect.

I was very glad for that experience, because several years later I had an African-American honors student who wanted to be an architect. When she came to me for advice, I was able to relay the story. She became a psychology major and art minor, and went on to become an excellent architect.

I firmly believe Christian students seeking degrees need to let God remold their minds. Christian students will have more career opportunities, and will better serve God, if they attend a university seeking knowledge, understanding, and wisdom.

Breaking the Mold

Hearing or reading that God wants Christians to be interested in knowledge, understanding, and wisdom is easy, but remolding a mind to live a life in pursuit of knowledge is not easy. The degree/job mold is a very strong force in America. If you are not already a Proverbial student, breaking the mold will take considerable effort.

Not everyone understands how strong societal pressures can be, and how difficult it is to change. To demonstrate, consider the pressures facing Copernicus and Galileo. Copernicus was a brilliant and influential man. He is probably best known for his theories related to astronomy.

The dominant view of the heavens during his time was that the sun rose in the east and circled the earth because the earth was the center of the universe. That view obviously agrees with what seems to happen and makes good sense. To direct experience, the sun rises in the east and goes down in the west. To believe differently requires abstract thought; an individual has to imagine the earth turning as it revolves around the sun.

Around 1514, Copernicus distributed a small treatise that suggested the earth was not the center of the universe. He proposed the earth was orbiting the sun. He knew the Roman Church was opposed to such a position at the time. The church believed Earth was the center of the universe. The gist of the opposition was that the sun could not be the center of the universe, because God sent his Son to earth to save us; therefore, we must be the center of the universe.

Some sixty years after Copernicus died, the church made an official statement against the heliocentric view of the universe. The idea that the earth moves and the sun does not was described as false and altogether opposed to Holy Scripture.

After 1610, Galileo began supporting Copernicus' views publicly. He met with bitter opposition from some clerics and was warned to abandon his support. When he defended his views he was tried and found suspect of heresy and spent the rest of his life under house arrest.

Think about what I am saying. Just a few hundred years ago, the very strong pressure of the church was for the sun to be circling the earth. The church threatened those who would think differently. People who went against the church and believed the earth is circling the sun were thought to be committing heresy. They faced severe consequences.

The pressures to pursue a degree rather than an education are not as life-threatening as the church was to Copernicus and Galileo, but the pressures are very strong. Peer pressure, parental pressure, the media forces, and other forces are strong. Remolding a mind takes work, discipline, and even courage. Remolding a mind into that of a Proverbial student is the narrow path—but the narrow path is worth the work.

Chapter 4

Be Curious about Ideas

"The wise man also may hear and increase in
learning and the man of understanding acquire skill
to understand a proverb and a figure, the words of
the wise and their riddles"

(Prov. 1:5–6).

To break the career mold and gain a good education, being
curious about ideas is critically important. Other factors
help an education, obviously. Intelligence is helpful, but
being highly intelligent is neither a necessary nor a sufficient
condition for someone to gain an education. You do not have
to be brilliant to be educated, and not all brilliant people are
educated.

I know many bright people who are not interested in an
education. Quite often, learning has come too easy for them.
They are bored by tedious classroom activities and studies geared
to average or below average students. They are not challenged
by excellent teachers. They get by, and even excel, grade-wise
without study or discipline. They meet low high-school stan-
dards with minimum effort. They beat a system, rather than
gain knowledge and understanding.

I also know many people of average intelligence who are serious about education. They may have to take a few more times through a book to gain knowledge; they may have to record lectures and review notes more frequently than other students; but they seek to gain knowledge and understanding. Consequently, they become educated people who apply knowledge and seek wisdom throughout their lives.

No matter what your level of intelligence is, in my opinion curiosity is a more important characteristic for wisdom than intelligence. A person of average intelligence with exceptional curiosity will gain a better education that a brilliant person without curiosity.

Curiosity about ideas is much more than memorizing facts for Trivial Pursuit or Jeopardy. Curiosity about ideas requires your interest in abstract thought. An interest in abstract ideas is a thoroughly Christian concept. Christ expected you to be engaged in abstract thought—he taught in parables. To understand parables requires the ability to think in abstractions.

Curiosity about abstract ideas can turn most of your university classes into enjoyable learning experiences. If you are curious about abstract ideas, if you are seeking to gain knowledge, you will not be bored in most classes. Unfortunately, many students are being molded by computers and television to expect entertainment in the classroom. Curiosity and gaining knowledge are not as important as feeling good.

Schools, teachers, and political systems bear some responsibility for the failure to develop curiosity. Very few programs are developed and implemented to make you accountable for being curious. The stress on standardized test scores dominates the K–12 system—a system that produces more motivated memorizers than students curious about knowledge.

I came to believe that if I assigned students a particular topic and asked them to produce a twenty-page, single-spaced paper, with exactly 150 words per page, and told them to read the paper to me on a Thursday at 4:17 pm, while standing on the twelfth step in front of the student union, they would easily and happily accomplish that assignment. But if I asked them to produce a two-page paper describing what they thought about a subject, or how they would attack a research problem or anything that demanded curiosity and abstract thought, most would be dumbfounded. The most frequent student response to a request for thought was "Tell me what you want me to do, and I will do it." When I told them to think, to be curious, many students failed to understand.

If you develop curiosity, you will seek to learn about the economic and political factors that shape your life. You will try to understand the social and psychological factors that make you and others behave. You will seek to understand ethics and logic. You will try to understand scientific knowledge that describes our world. And yes, you will seek to gain the knowledge that will help you in your career.

In the following chapters I will use three topics to demonstrate the fun and importance of being curious: context, free will/determinism, and decision-making. I will show how gaining knowledge, and thinking with that knowledge, develops understanding—and hopefully, wisdom.

Chapter 5

Context

"It is not good for a man to be without knowledge"

(Prov. 19:2).

I wish I could be present to convey my excitement to anyone who undertakes the process of becoming a Proverbial student. Remolded minds are never bored; you find excitement in life and contribute to society. Being curious about knowledge strengthens a person's faith. If you choose to begin the remolding process, begin with prayer for understanding. In addition to prayer, I encourage you to develop curiosity.

For years, I taught students the importance of the first idea I will be presenting. I am enthusiastic about it because it has meant so much to my students. Years after they graduated, many former students reported how this idea started them toward an education and helped them gain knowledge and understanding. I pray you have a similar experience.

The idea I want you to ponder is *context*.

"Point of view" and "frame of reference" are two good synonyms for this. If this were a philosophical essay, I might spend several pages parsing differences in meaning for various terms, but for present purposes a general understanding of context is sufficient.

Thinking about context increases knowledge and understanding of your world—and can be fun at the same time! Understanding the importance of context, and of thinking with various contexts, will help lead to paths of understanding and wisdom. I pray that having fun and thinking with the idea will increase your curiosity and help you follow the narrow path to becoming a Proverbial student.

Knowing Context Helps Understanding

A fun and easy way to demonstrate the importance of context is to read the following paragraph:

> The procedure is actually quite simple. First you arrange things into different groups depending upon their makeup. Of course, one pile may be sufficient depending on how much there is to do. If you have to go somewhere because of the lack of facilities that is the next step, otherwise you are pretty well set. It is important not to overdue any particular endeavor. That is, it is better to do too few things than too many. In the short run this may not seem too important, but complications from doing too many things can easily arise. A mistake can be expensive as well. The manipulation of the appropriate mechanism should be self-explanatory, and we need not dwell on it here. At first the whole procedure will seem complicated. Soon however, it will become just another fact of life. It is difficult to foresee any end to the necessity for this task in the immediate future, but then one can never tell.[1]

When I read that paragraph to students, a lot of head-shaking and eye-rolling occurs. When I asked them what was being talked about, some invented answers because they were afraid to say "I do not know." Most students just looked bewildered. The truth is you do not know what is being talked about. The paragraph is gobbledygook without a context.

However, when I give two words to establish a context or frame of reference, the paragraph almost magically makes sense. The two words are: *washing clothes*! Reread the paragraph and see how easily the gobbledygook is turned into understanding with the proper context.

In addition to increased knowledge and understanding, research has clearly shown that the ability to recall information is greatly increased when the context is known and understood. If you just attend class and try to memorize coursework for some test without context, you will find that most classes quickly become gobbledygook. If, however, you seek to understand the context for the information and seek to gain knowledge within the context, the ideas will be easier to learn and easier to retain.

Knowing the context a university professor uses will increase your ability to gain knowledge and understanding. Some teachers' perspectives will be antithetical to Christian perspectives. You do not have to agree with a teacher's context, but knowing that context will help learning. With the grace of God, you will be given the wisdom to choose between right views and the wrong ones.

A Proverbial student should easily start to see the importance of context for knowledge and understanding. A curious student wants to know more about context and its implications. I always gave several examples—still trying to make it fun, but also showing how knowledge of one idea can greatly expand understanding across a wide variety of topics.

Even Elementary Ideas Are Learned within a Context

To encourage further curiosity and broaden understanding about context, answer one simple question: How much is 1 + 1?

Most people answer "2," and clearly they are correct in a particular context. But, is another answer possible?

Consider the same question in a different context. "In a sense, what is the most frequent answer to 1 + 1 on a daily basis in the United States of America?" Is the only answer 2? Are other answers possible?

My hope is you will be curious, think outside of the box, and imagine a different answer.

Even the most elementary knowledge has been learned within a particular context, which for 1 + 1 is Base 10. However, most addition is done in computers, and most computers operate in Base 2. Base 2 is a system with only two symbols: 1 and 0. Counting is done with only two symbols; thus, you have 0, 1, 10, 11, 100, 101, 110, 111, etc. Addition and other operations are performed with two, and only two, symbols. Therefore, in a clear sense, 1 + 1 in a computer is 10 (one, zero).

In my class discussions, a few students were totally lost. A few understood when I explained Base 2; most students knew I was right but were not sure about Base 2; a few thought I was crazy. A few thought I was one of those liberal communist teachers their parents and pastors had warned them about. They had memorized 1 + 1 on their flash cards. The answer 2 was good enough for the first grade in their hometown and, by God, the answer was going to stay 2.

My concern here is not proficiency in mathematical bases. This is not a math book. My hope is that you realize that even very simple information—information as simple as 1 + 1—is learned within a context (Base 10), and that realization will make you curious and excited about new knowledge and deeper understanding. Thankfully, most of my students reacted in that manner. I hope you will also.

Understanding the frame of references through which you have gained knowledge will increase understanding, and by the grace of God, make you wiser. Isn't that better than memorizing for the next test?

I enjoyed teaching this and other related ideas, because understanding the importance of context opens minds to new opportunities; one clear example concerns a former student who lived with us and our daughter.

A few years ago, our daughter was on her way to work, when a trash truck ran a stop sign and hit her; she was killed instantly. She had earned her BS and master's in physics. She was very successful because she gained scientific knowledge and could also communicate it in ways that engineers and scientists understood, as well as communicate that information to laborers and executives.

Many people reached out to us in our grief. One of them had lived in Christian community with us when I taught at Illinois State University. He wrote how fondly he remembered her and related a story from that time.

During one of our supper discussions, I went into my discussion of context, using Base 2 as my example. He did not understand what I was saying. He was befuddled, but he was embarrassed to ask questions.

Our daughter stayed with him at the dinner table after everyone left, and patiently our eleven-year-old explained context and Base 2 to him, the college student—ideas she had heard many times. She did not make him feel stupid, and he was very grateful. I am delighted to note that he went from not understanding anything about Base 2 to having a very successful career in the use of computers for business and education. His mind had been remolded.

Avoid Narrow-mindedness

Implicit in the discussion thus far is the idea that other contexts are possible for most events and ideas. Taxes are reported in

Base 10, but other bases are possible. Understanding that other contexts are possible should broaden your understanding and open your mind to new possibilities.

Being aware of new possibilities is good for Christians, with the understanding that every new possibility is not necessarily an appropriate choice for a Christian. All contexts are not correct choices, but being narrow-minded restricts the ability to gain knowledge, to gain understanding, and to be wise. A wise person knows alternatives and makes informed choices; a narrow-minded person usually is limited to doing what has been done to him or her.

Long before the movie *Glory Road* made Don Haskins known to the modern generation I discussed him in my classes. I asked students what basketball game had the biggest effect on their learning environment. Most students had no idea how the racial implications of the Texas Western (today UTEP) versus Kentucky in the NCAA Division I men's basketball title game in 1966 changed the makeup of sports teams and student populations in southern universities. (If you are not aware of that game, Texas Western was the first team to start five black players in a Division I championship game. They handily defeated the all-white University of Kentucky team—forever changing the landscape of athletic teams, and consequently racial enrollment patterns, in many schools.)

My point about knowing other contexts are possible involves Don Haskins' nickname. Throughout the United States he was known as "Bear" Haskins. His size and appearance made it an appropriate nickname.

Toward the end of his career he had a good team and was advancing in the NCAA men's basketball championship. He and his team were receiving substantial publicity. I told my students about a letter to the editor I read in *USA Today*. In the letter, someone wrote in that it was inappropriate to call him Bear Haskins because there was only one "Bear"—an obvious reference to Bear Bryant, the beloved former football coach for the University of Alabama.

I asked the students to guess in which state the narrow-minded letter writer was living; they had no trouble knowing it was Alabama. I wanted them to see that having only one context for a nickname was so narrow-minded as to appear stupid. Since I was teaching in Alabama, I was quick to assure them that if they or their parents or their grandparents wanted to love Bear Bryant with all their hearts, minds, souls, and strength and have no other Bears before him, that was quite well and good—but to please have the understanding and wisdom to see that other Bears are possible.

I have numerous examples showing obvious problems with being narrow-minded. Another favorite involves the metric system. Several years ago, metric signs began to appear along our interstate highways. Because I was steeped in the US Customary System, I was glad for the signs. The information helped me begin to develop an elementary understanding of metric distances.

However, the metric mileage signs did not last long and were removed from the interstate highways. Some politicians argued that the attempt to teach the metric system was an attempt to get us to adopt a foreign system as a part of a plan to have a one-world political system. The only context for measurement that they knew and understood was the US Customary System. The metric system was foreign. They rejected the foreign system.

Obviously the politicians were not well educated in science or mathematics. With a good education, they would have had a scientific context and mathematical context for the metric system. Not only is another context for measurement possible, it is advantageous for many operations. I doubt that those same politicians, when they ran to the foreign car companies with tax breaks trying to attract them to Alabama, ever demanded that the companies get rid of their metric wrenches.

Correct Answers Often Depend on Context

Implicit in this discussion is the idea that any answer often depends on context. As you gain wisdom, you will learn how often you can intelligently respond to a question with "It depends," because many answers depend on context.

Most of the time, a common context is understood. Details of the context do not have to be delineated to know the correct answer, such as using Base 10. However, at other times, context must be taken into account to determine the correct answer.

For example, take the question: "Who discovered America?" Usually, students give one answer: Christopher Columbus. Many are familiar with the little ditty, "Columbus sailed the ocean blue in fourteen hundred and ninety-two." But if you understand my point about context, you realize that different answers are possible. Who discovered America from a southern European perspective? Christopher Columbus. There is nothing wrong with that answer. However, who discovered America from the perspective of a northern European? Evidence suggests the Vikings and fishermen of the Scandinavian countries were in America even before Columbus. From an anthropological perspective, the Native Americans were here when Columbus arrived, so their ancestors obviously "discovered America" before Columbus. A student needs to know the context to know which answer is correct.

A word of caution: Different contexts can provide different answers, but just because different contexts are possible does not mean all contexts provide correct answers. Too many students, when they first begin to understand context, adopt the attitude, "You have your position, and I have mine; both are correct." That is true for some matters, but for others one context clearly provides the best answer. In matters of faith, some people adopt the context that God does not exist and that guides their values. As Christians, we have a different context for our lives—and both cannot be correct.

A Practical Application for College Students

I could have chosen to challenge you with any number of major ideas. I chose context because it is fun to think with, applies to many situations, and in addition has a very practical application, which we'll look at now.

One practical problem faced by students is managing reading assignments. To try to help students, early in my classes I always asked: "The first time through Chapter 1, how long did it take you to read the chapter?" Some students were honest and acknowledged they had not started to read. Many indicated they spent quite a bit of time studying but were not through reading the first chapter. Most described the process as getting out their highlighters and trying to memorize the chapter word for word, sentence by sentence, paragraph by paragraph.

Very, very few students reported reading in the best manner, as suggested by very good research. The first time through a chapter, you should take a few minutes to scan a section or a chapter for the main points. A clear notion of the outline and the main points should be established. Then, the main ideas should be kept in mind as each chapter is read in more detail.

Most authors write from an outline of the most important points; the largest ideas in the outline create the chapters. More detailed information is presented within the outline for each chapter. Often textbook authors stress the outline for each chapter by listing the main ideas at the start of each chapter. They repeat the stress by putting each big individual idea in large boldface type at the start of each section that develops each idea.

Despite the best efforts of authors to get students' attention by giving an outline of the important topics for each chapter, most students skip the outline. Despite the best efforts of authors to get students' attention by highlighting the outline in enormous type at the start of each section, most students skip over the large type. Students entirely miss the context for their reading assignments.

Scanning for the main points and knowing the outline establishes a context. Authors write with the expectation that you will have the context in mind as you read the details.

An easy demonstration of bad reading habits is to ask students, "What is the chapter title for Chapter 1?" and "What are the major sections in Chapter 1?" When I ask those questions, students are dumbfounded. They believe I am asking unfair questions. Yet, if I ask for a trivial detail located on page 7, they are apt to know it.

Quite often, good students spend less time reading than other students because they read with the context in mind. Because of their ability to establish context, comprehension is much faster and better. Other students try to memorize all of the details and are quickly overwhelmed—or worse, quit trying. They wear out their highlighters and are perplexed when students who spend less time reading perform better on exams.

Proverbial students should take advantage of the knowledge we have about reading. Knowing the context before reading details helps comprehension and retention. You would be wise to read accordingly.

Similarly, class notes should be organized into the main ideas and the details for those ideas. Sometimes when I tried to help students, I asked to see their notes. For weaker students, the notes would often be a series of statements without a context. They were not organized into main points. The students missed the context and organization the teacher was presenting. Rather than seeing a lecture as four main ideas with twenty details about each idea, students saw eighty individual topics.

Learn to listen, as well as read, with the context in mind. It is much easier to remember to learn twenty details related to four ideas than eighty separate details.

Context and Faith Issues

Context also has important implications for understanding many faith issues. An important one is our understanding of other cultures and other people.

God clearly calls us to care for others. When asked to summarize the commandments, Christ made it clear: We are to love the Lord our God with all of our heart, mind, soul, and strength, and have to no other gods before him. We are to love our neighbors as ourselves. Context is a very important idea for understanding and loving others, and for defining who our neighbors are.

All too often we are unaware of the context of others' lives. Even worse, we may be aware of another person's context but arrogantly and incorrectly think of our context as the only way. Such a self-righteous attitude hurts our relationships with other people.

A clear example of assuming "our way is the only way" occurred in my Learning class. I always showed students the extensive power of our minds for visual images, using a zoo example. I randomly went around the room and asked students to name an animal. We mentally imagined the animals being someplace in the room. The zoo usually contained up to twenty animals.

A few days later, I would ask the class how many of them took notes listing the animals and studying them. Usually, no one had given the animals a second thought. Without rehearsal, however, the class was usually able to easily reconstruct the vast majority of the zoo. Our minds have enormous capacities for visual information.

Stuart was one of my favorite students. He was my advisee and took several classes from me. When I asked him to name an animal, he said "zeb-ra"—pronouncing "zeb" as in "deb" or "reb" rather than zee-bra. I asked him to repeat what he'd said, and he repeated the word with the same pronunciation, adding, "You know, the horse-like animal with black and white stripes."

The class laughed at his strange pronunciation. Since their context for pronunciation was zebra with a long e, he was obviously wrong.

Stuart then asked a very good question: "How many of you are from a country where zeb-ras are native to the country?" You could have heard a pin drop. Stuart was from South Africa. Zebras are native to his country. His pronunciation was perfectly appropriate.

Stuart's pronunciation is but one small example where we believe our context is either the only way or the right way. You can easily expand this example to see why we often have trouble witnessing to other cultures when we insist on our context being the correct and only way.

One of the most entertaining ways to try to understand the importance of other contexts is to watch the movie *Dead Poets Society*. In the movie, Robin Williams portrays a teacher who at the last minute is hired to teach English to young white boys at a New England prep school. By various means, he tries to get his students to see that other contexts are possible for their lives. (I encourage everyone to watch the movie, and learn the various ways he demonstrates the importance of context.) One of my favorite scenes is when he asks students to get up from their desks, come to the front of the room, stand up on the teacher's desk, turn around and face the class. It presented the students with a very different perspective than sitting erect and proper in neat little rows. It was a dramatic and effective way to challenge students to see other contexts.

As a sad irony, consider the following observations: After a class discussion of the movie, I had one student come up and say he would not watch the movie because he heard it was about boys reading poetry. Obviously his view of masculinity did not include boys reading poetry and, unfortunately, he was not about to change his mind. His context for masculinity was fixed, and an education would not change his mind. His understanding of others, and consequently his ability to love others, was scarred by such a narrow context. If he had realized and accepted other contexts for masculinity, he would have had an increased ability to love as Jesus would have us love.

Another observation was that very few black students reported seeing the movie. In my discussions with them, they often implied or stated the movie only contained meaning for white people; therefore, they did not need to see it. Again, I was sad that a narrow frame of reference for some members of one racial community meant that such an important message was lost to them.

My sadness about narrow racial views is not restricted to blacks. When I first moved to Alabama and learned that some children were not allowed to watch Bill Cosby on television because he was black, I was stunned. Such narrow-mindedness is not tolerable for a Christian.

I strongly believe racial attitudes are changing for the better, but change would occur quicker if we had knowledge, understanding, and wisdom about the contexts shaping each other's lives. We would be better able to express Christian love if we understood the contexts for each other's lives: black, brown, white, and all combinations in between.

Martin was an international student from Honduras who my wife and I have aided in several ways over the years. He came to the university as a member of an international studies program and spent two years completing his undergraduate studies. He was a frequent guest in our home; he was a student in my classes, an advisee, and remains a friend to this day.

When he finished his studies, my wife and I paid for his mother to be present for Martin's graduation. I still remember the lengthy amount of time she spent washing her hair because she did not have ready access to a lengthy shower in her home (another contextual issue).

As we sat down that last day before Martin left to return home, I asked him, "What about your experience has been good? Has anything been a disappointment?" I was mostly interested in learning how we could make the experience better for any future international students. Martin listed several very good aspects about the program. His one disappointment greatly surprised me: He was greatly disappointed in his inability to form relationships with our black students. Several of his best friends in Honduras were Garifuna—among the "blackest" people in the world.

Martin had repeatedly tried to greet and be friendly to Southern black students on our campus, and was repeatedly rebuffed. As soon as they saw he was Hispanic, he felt they ignored him, or were short with him. The black students he encountered had a context for friendship that did not include close relationships between blacks and Hispanics.

I will never be able to adopt or completely understand an African-American, Hispanic, or Asian-American context because I am white. But I can try, and the more I understand the better we are able to relate. The same is true for other cultures trying to understand me.

Even more important to my faith is the ability to seek and understand Christian contexts that transcend race and culture. As Christians, we are told to make no distinction between races, gender, cultures, economic status, etc. I take that to mean that our values should have a higher context. If you are Asian, black, Hispanic, or white, you have different lives than people of other races and cultures. But if you understand that other contexts are possible, your education can lead to Christian contexts which can be common to all races and cultures. Christian understanding does not deny individual experiences or different cultural contexts, but Christian values transcend other contexts.

For example, valuing love should be common to all cultures. In truth, all the fruit of the Spirit should be important values in life no matter the race, gender, or culture. With God's help, everyone should be striving to be filled with love, joy, peace, patience, kindness, gentleness, tolerance, generosity, strength, and self-control, no matter an individual's background or culture.

One particularly revealing incident about cultural differences occurred in a Sunday school class my wife and I taught for college students. In class was an international student who had a distinctly different body odor from the other students. Some members of the class had asked us to speak to him about the odor.

Before we said anything to him, a revealing incident occurred. One Sunday he came to the class with a request: If our class would raise a small amount of money (less than one student often spent on a weekend of fun) he could buy enough PVC pipe for his village to run water from a spring to their village two miles away. The pipe would save the villagers having to walk four miles each day, the last two miles carrying their heavy loads of water.

Many of the class realized, probably for the first time, that not everyone has the resources to take showers without regard to the amount of water being used. Also, not everyone could afford the costly perfumes, deodorants, and cologne they took for granted. While the odor was still uncomfortable to some, the class quickly and more lovingly adopted a different context for viewing our friend.

I took the occasion to try to teach some of the students more about context by explaining that in the not-too-distant past, body odor was thought to be appealing in certain cultures. Some Christians rejected bathing, because they associated it with the sin of pride and vanity. As we learned the importance of hygiene for health, our views about baths and odor changed. Our context for odors clearly influenced how we "sensed" each other.

Clearly, if an idea can give you better understanding of others, it can give you better wisdom in our faith. Context is such an idea. I hope you as Proverbial students will use it to help you love others as you love yourself.

In addition to practical Christian actions, context helps theological and philosophical understanding. Understanding context means understanding that some "truths" are relative to context. Many of my more conservative students struggle with the idea that some truths are relative. Many pastors and parents warn students about relativism. They dismiss or belittle university professors who teach relativism because they think relativism implies no absolute truths. They believe absolute truths are to be found solely in their interpretations of the Bible, and any talk of relativism is denying the authority of Holy Scripture.

To say that some knowledge is relative (as I am saying) is not the same as saying *all* knowledge is relative. To say that most knowledge is relative is not to deny some absolute truths. To claim that there are *only* absolute truths is silly. Unfortunately, too many students are quick to hold that position. They show the same narrow-mindedness that led the church to threaten Copernicus for heretical claims that Earth is revolving around the sun.

As knowledge of context is better understood, a Proverbial student thinks with understanding. Rather than just agreeing with a position expressed in a book because a friend or a pastor or a counselor recommended it, you would be able to think about your theological positions and agree or disagree with understanding—a sign of wisdom.

Understanding context can also help you to understand theological arguments. I recently discussed context with my interim minister. In one of her theology classes, she was reading a book stressing a different context for the parables—to read the parables as Christ speaking to oppressed people, not as stories with a moral.

As I talked with her, I acknowledged I could read the parables from different viewpoints such as liberation theology, but I did not believe that was necessarily the only context for reading the parables. Also, just because I could read them with a different understanding did not mean I necessarily agreed with an alternative perspective. To me, if someone accepts liberation theology as the only way to read the parables, they are being as narrow-minded as the church with Copernicus. I believe God's Holy Spirit allows and enables many uses of parables, and seeing and understanding different contexts for reading them is helpful. Whether or not a person agrees with liberation theology is not of major importance for present purposes. Understanding how the concept of context can help theological understanding is the point.

A final critically important relationship of context to faith issues is the role it plays in reading and understanding the Bible. Recently I attended a retreat, and had the pleasure of gaining knowledge from an excellent biblical scholar. I clearly remember him saying,

"If you do not remember anything else, always remember the three most important factors for understanding Scripture: The first is context. The second is context. And the third is context."

In order to have clear and accurate interpretations of Scripture you need to know the context for what you are reading. To whom was it written? Under what conditions was it written? What did the words and ideas mean at the time and place they were written?

Context, context, context!

In many classes, teachers will adopt contexts that are challenging, even antithetical, to a Christian perspective. Those views may be conservative, or they may be liberal. A Proverbial student will seek to understand the contexts. Please be careful: I did not say *accept* them; I said *understand* them. Understanding other contexts will strengthen your understanding of your own views.

As a result of becoming a Proverbial student, some personal theological views may change. In my life, most of my changes have broadened and deepened my faith. Change has not taken me further from Christ but closer to him. These changes have enabled me to be wiser in my relationships with other people and to better understand Scripture. I pray that the same occurs for you.

Summary

The breadth of knowledge about context and its applications are extensive. The thinking student should note that my examples included mathematics/statistics, education/reading, international studies, computer science, history, athletics, social issues, theology, and certainly psychology. I could have given more examples in other disciplines. Gaining knowledge about context will increase understanding across many academic areas for the Proverbial student.

Chapter 6

Where There's a Will

"Free will is important, but an informed
will leads to wise decisions"

(personal proverb).

Our next topic is just as deep, broad, and intellectually important as context.

When I fly, I like to read popular novels, typically mysteries. I usually read them within the context of entertainment, but sometimes I cannot escape deeper implications. One of my favorite authors is Sue Grafton, who developed a series of fun mystery books that I find interesting and easy reads—each of which has a letter of the alphabet in the title. She started her series with *A Is for Alibi*. As of 2010 she was up to *U Is for Undertow*, which begins with the following paragraph:

What fascinates me about life is that now and then the past rises up and declares itself. Afterward, the sequence of events seems inevitable, but only because cause and effect had been aligned in advance. It's like a pattern of dominoes arranged upright on a tabletop. With the flick of your finger, the first tile topples on

the second, which in turn tips into the third setting
in motion a tumbling that goes on and on, each
tile knocking over its neighbor until all of them fall
down. Sometimes the impetus is pure chance, though
I discount the notion of accidents. Fate stitches
together elements that seem unrelated on the surface.
It is only when the truth emerges you see how the
bones are joined and everything connects.[2]

Of course the book can be read for pure entertainment,
but a Proverbial student would also clearly understand that
in a philosophical context, Grafton is touching on one of
the most important ideas a thoughtful person can ponder:
the issue of free will vs. determinism. I have had great
pleasure and success getting students to gain knowledge and
understanding by having them intellectually wrestle this big,
important topic.

Most students have a superficial acceptance of the basic
ideas of free will. When I challenge their simplistic acceptance,
they typically have a good time expanding their knowledge by
thinking and struggling with the new concepts. Certainly the
topic is an outstanding example of the fun and energy that can
develop from thinking and the pursuit of knowledge.

I introduce the topic with a few questions; if students have
curiosity, then the intellectual wrestling begins in earnest. One
of my favorite opening questions is, "How many of you have
free will?" Everyone will raise their hand. I usually say something
like, "That was not very enthusiastic; let me see you raise your
hands a little higher." They do.

Next I ask, "How many of you are controlled?" Most
students are a little puzzled by the question, and either do not

raise their hands or reluctantly raise them. I continue, "You are not controlled because you have free will?" They nod.

Then the fun begins. I ask: "If you are not controlled, why did you raise your hands when I asked you a question? Why did you raise them higher when I asked you to raise your hands higher?" At this point I have their attention—and we begin an enjoyable and far-reaching interaction.

Some very famous philosophers spent much of their lives reflecting and writing tomes about the free-will/determinism issue. I am not about to develop a lot of technical detail, but I do want to point out a few basic important tenets to get you to think.

First, a few common-sense definitions: On one extreme of the debate are people who believe everything has causes and that free will is an illusion. In short, free will does not exist. Determinism (or total determinism) is a name for that position.

At the other extreme are people who believe they are not controlled in any way. They can do anything they want, when they want, and however they want. They believe they have total free will.

In between would be the people who accept that some behavior is caused, while at the same time asserting that free will exists. The hard work is determining the limits of the two.

Physicists and others have argued whether all actions have causes. In that context, it is probably more accurate to call the debate a determinism/non-determinism debate, since it is difficult to assign free will to inanimate or non-human objects.

The debate covers the action of all objects, but is argued most fervently regarding human behavior. We are more engaged with the debate as it applies to humans, where free will makes intuitive sense.

A very important distinction is the difference between fatalism and determinism. Fatalism is the view that no matter what I do, such and such will happen. What is meant to be, will be. Fate cannot be controlled.

Determinism is the view that if certain causes occur, then particular events will follow. Causes control events.

War gives a common-sense way to understand the distinction between fatalism and determinism. In the movies and other stories, soldiers are said to believe the following: "If my name is on a bullet, nothing I can do will prevent my death; when my time comes, there is nothing I can do to prevent my death." A silly corollary is to believe that I can take great risks because unless a bullet has my name I will not get killed; and if it does have my name I am going to die no matter what. That is fatalism at its best or worst, depending on your view.

Determinists, on the other hand, believe that if I raise my head when people are shooting at me, I have a greater chance of being shot than if I am hiding behind something—so I keep my head down. Bullets will not defy the laws of physics to find me.

One more distinction is important: Freedom is not the same as free will. Freedom is the number of perceived choices you have, while free will is the ability to make choices. For example, assume a person chooses to smoke and that he or she can select from four brands of cigarettes. A second person can choose from twenty brands. Both people have the same *free will* to choose to smoke or not to smoke; the latter person has more *freedom* than the first. Whether or not a person has free will in a situation, increased freedom is good and valuable, as long as people accept the responsibility for the consequences of their choices.

Most students have a ready acceptance of free will and have given very little thought to how they may be controlled by their genes or their environment. People tend to lean toward the intellectual position that most behavior is a matter of free will. They have a simple acceptance of the view and have never considered otherwise. They believe it to be true and that is good enough. They have never considered the problems with formal proof of a position.

Since most students have a naive acceptance and have not constructed arguments for their free-will position, I challenge that naivety in order to get them to think. As you review the following questions and discussion, always remember that my position on the issue is not known. Just because I am raising questions about the free-will position does not mean I am a total determinist. As a teacher, I am trying to get you to think about your views.

The free will/determinism debate is not about fatalism or the amount of freedom, or number of choices, but about the possibility of causes for choices people make. If the environment causes a person to make a particular choice, then their behavior is being caused. If the choices are not caused, then behaviors should be random. Again, the habit of smoking is a good topic for discussing free will/determinism.

In my classes I ask students, "How many of you smoke? Do you smoke of your own free will? Are there any factors that cause you to choose or not choose a particular brand?"

After they think about their answers I ask them, "How many men smoke Virginia Slims? How many women smoke Camels without a filter?"

The students may exercise their free will to choose to smoke or not to smoke; but even in that choice the presence or absence of smoking in their family, health issues, financial issues, and many more factors usually play a role in their choices. If they choose to smoke, another set of factors play a role in determining which cigarettes they choose to smoke. Advertisers work very hard to influence people to buy one brand over another.

Before the idea of control is dismissed as silly because people can choose what they want, consider the life of one of the founding fathers of American psychology, John B. Watson. Watson was a noted behaviorist and believed all behavior was caused. He was a total determinist. When he was fired from his academic job, he put his philosophy into practice. He went into advertising and successfully designed ways to influence people to buy products.

Another fun topic is individuality. Most students believe they exercise free will by being different from others. They believe tattoos, earrings, hairstyles, styles of dress, ways of talking, and any number of behaviors are exercises of their free will.

My challenge to them comes from one of my favorite venues: cartoons. I love cartoons because in order to be a good cartoonist, the cartoonist has to be a great observer of behavior. One of the best and most longstanding cartoons is *Blondie*. The challenge for students is found in a dialogue between Dagwood and his son:

The son comes to Dagwood and says, "I want to get an earring."

Dagwood responds, "No son of mine is going to wear an earring!"

The son replies, "But Dad, I want to be different"—followed by the critical phrase, "just like all of my friends."

I want to be different—just like all of my friends. He is not being an individual; he is not exercising free will; he is shaped by his friends. I loved to challenge the students who thought they were exercising free will by being different. I loved to show them that people with purple hair tend to be around other people with tinted hair. People who dress in Goth style hang out with others who dress in Goth style. A minority group can be just as conforming as a majority group.

If a student does not believe me, my ultimate challenge is for the students to change hair styles or dress styles and see the reaction of their peers. A Goth need only show up in a suit and tie, or Nike athletic wear, and watch the reaction of his or her peer group to see how strong peer pressure is within group norms.

The free will/determinism debate is a deep and wide concern in many areas. The thinking student will easily find this topic present in many academic disciplines:

Philosophy. Kant and many other major philosophers have written extensively about it.

Physics. Newton's third law of motion states that for every action there is an equal and opposite reaction. Two of the biggest names in Physics, Bohr and Einstein, debated the issue in quantum mechanics. They considered: Is it possible for very small measurements to be made without influencing the measurements?

Biology. Are Brownian movements random or caused?

Mathematics. The study of fractals and chaos theory has implications for determinism/nondeterminism.

Art. Interestingly, Picasso argued that he was a determinist because everything he did stood on the shoulders of those who went before him; other artists scream that their works are acts of free will.

Poetry/Literature. In addition to the Grafton quote previously given, consider a quote from another popular writer and

62   Being a Proverbial Student

favorite of mine, Tony Hillerman. In *Dance Hall of the Dead*, he reflects about the Navajo religion:

> "When the dung beetle moves," Hosteen Nashibbitti had told him, "know that something has moved it. And know that its movement affects the flight of the sparrow, and that the raven deflects the eagle from the sky, and that the eagle's stiff wing bends the will of the wind people, and know that all of this affects you and me, and the flea on the prairie dog and the leaf on the cottonwood." That had always been the point of the lesson.

> Interdependency of nature; every cause has its effect; every action its reaction; a reason for everything. In all things a pattern, and in this pattern the beauty of harmony. Thus one learned to live with evil by understanding it, by reading its cause. And thus one learned, gradually and methodically, if one was lucky, to always "go in beauty," to always look for the pattern, and to find it.[3]

Psychology and Sociology. Is behavior caused? Obviously causal relationships are central themes of both disciplines.

Political Science. Any consideration about responsibility for human actions, as well as debates about punishment vs. rehabilitation, will have to consider issues related to the determinism/free will debate.

The importance of the free will/determinism debate is critically important in applied disciplines. The concept of management implies an administrator's behavior causes certain job performance. Advertising and public relations depend on people responding according to known relationships. Nursing, medicine, engineering, criminal justice, and other applied disciplines all depend on causal relationships. Assume you go to a doctor who says, "Take this medicine, it may or it may not work." I certainly would not pay for a medicine with random results.

Imagine a child has a problem and the parents visit two psychologists. One says, "Your child has this problem, but we will just have to hope that she will of her own free will decide to behave differently." The second says, "We do not have all of the answers and we cannot force her to behave in a certain way, but if we do these things we have evidence that we will increase the chances that she will overcome the problem." Which therapist are the parents going to continue to see?

As with context, the free will/determinism issue has important implications for faith issues. Examine the differences between the views of Free-will Baptists and Presbyterians, and you will find the importance of the debate. The topic is critical for theological positions on major social issues, such as: Are gays born gay, or do they choose to be gay by their free will? The list could go on and on and on and on.

Obviously the free will/determinism debate is an important intellectual topic for many disciplines. A Proverbial student needs to gain knowledge about the debate. This knowledge will clearly deepen your understanding in your chosen career.

A wise person will go further. A wise person understands that a person may have free will but wisdom comes from an *informed* will. Gaining knowledge of known relationships deepens understanding and leads to wiser decisions.

Chapter 7

Decision-Making

———

"Wisdom abides in the mind of a man of understanding, but it is not known in the
heart of fools"

(Prov. 14:33).

My third topic to encourage the development of curiosity is decision-making. The topic is important in most academic disciplines. It is important for gaining knowledge, clearly deepens understanding, and is critical for wisdom. The failure to have decision-making skills is a major source of muddled thinking. Proverbial students are clear thinkers, not muddled thinkers.

I have a reoccurring nightmare about muddled thinking. My brother was a food flavor chemist, and took part of major decisions about the development of new food products. The decision to develop and market a new food product was not a ten-dollar decision; rather, it was often a several-million-dollar decision.

In my nightmare, several people are sitting around a table making a multimillion dollar decision about whether to develop a new food product such as a particular cookie. In my dream, one person says, "The cost analysis research and statistics show. . . ." A second person says, "The marketing research and statistics show. . . ." This process goes around the table with each person giving data, research, and statistics to determine a recommendation. They are clear thinkers.

One of my Christian students is the last person at the table. When the discussion comes to him (or her) the response goes something like this: "I never took a research course; I do not understand or care about statistics; I just really, really, really like this chip." At this point, I wake up in a cold sweat. My Christian student is a muddled (and soon to be unemployed) thinker.

A wise person understands logic, research, and statistical decision-making in order to make and understand many decisions. Data and statistics are not available for every decision, but when available they greatly help you make a knowledgeable, wise decision.

All too often I hear people boldly proclaim, "I do not believe in statistics; you can show anything you want to show with statistics." Or similarly," I do not believe in statistics because people lie with statistics." Neither of these proclamations are the claims of knowledgeable, wise people. Usually, they are being offered by people who want to persuade me to believe as they do, because they claim to be experts. Such an approach is ignorance, not wisdom.

My reply to the first statement is, "You cannot show anything you want with statistics to me; the statement is nonsense. For example, no one can use statistics to show me the average age of a person in America is seven years old. Or similarly it is impossible to show the average income in America is 1 million dollars per person."

A person can try to show me something using biased statistics, but the critical point is: *The more you understand statistics, the harder it is to mislead you.* That is a serious argument for understanding statistics and research, not for avoiding the field. The more knowledge you have about research and statistics, the better you are able to understand what others are claiming and to make your own decisions about those claims.

To the second statement I say, "Yes people lie with statistics. People also lie with the English language. Is that an argument to stop using the English language?"

A person can try to lie to me using statistics but the same critical point applies: *The more you understand statistics, the harder it is to lie to you.* Again, knowing the difference between truth and a lie is a serious argument for understanding research and statistics, not for avoiding the field.

Knowledge of research and statistics is particularly important for a Christian. We know some answers are matters of faith and belief. Logic, research, and statistics are not available or possible in all situations. But a wise person should have the knowledge of research and statistics, because they can help in making wise decisions when the knowledge is available.

Understanding research and statistics will enable you to understand when steps of faith or leaps of belief are being taken, and enable you to know the limits of your decisions. At the same time, you will not lose your job because you can knowledgeably sit at the decision-making table.

One has only to see the babble on the Internet to see the importance of research and statistical knowledge. I have a dear friend who sends me repeated warnings about our political situation, our history, and our future. She firmly believes the information because she gets it from trusted friends. With even a minimal amount of research, I repeatedly find the information is mistaken. She depends on friendship and experience for her knowledge. I also listen to friends and base many decisions on my own experience, but whenever it is available and appropriate, I use research and statistics to aid me in my decision-making.

A recent example has been played out in the press. Recent research has been performed on bracelets that are supposed to aid in balance and performance. The sale of those items is a multimillion dollar business. The research is clear: There is no support for the claims. When the proper research is performed, the bracelet does not improve balance or performance.

Despite the evidence, person after person will continue to buy the bracelet because they have a friend who "swears by them." A Proverbial student would gather knowledge and make a wise decision.

Although experimentation is not stressed in the Bible, we have a clear foundation for research in the story of Gideon and the fleece:

> Then Gideon said to God, "If thou wilt deliver Israel by my hand as thou hast said, behold I am laying a fleece of wool on the threshing floor; if there is dew on the fleece alone, and it is dry on all the ground, then I shall know that thou wilt deliver Israel by my hand as thou hast said." And it was so. When he rose early the next morning and squeezed the fleece, he wrung enough dew from the fleece to fill a bowl with water. Then Gideon said to God, "Let not thy anger burn against me, let me speak but this once with the fleece; pray, let it be dry only on the fleece, and all the ground let there be dew." And God did so that night;

for it was dry on the fleece only and on the ground all around there was dew (Jdgs. 6:36–40).

Gideon conducted research. He knew that if conditions were the same and the results were the opposite, only God could make that happen.

In experimentation, researchers try to hold all conditions the same except for one variable. If different results occur, they believe they are caused by the difference in the conditions. Scientists may not be interested in results that demonstrate God as was Gideon, but both are using research for answers.

I certainly encourage you to develop knowledge of logic, research, and statistics. Just as with context and free will/determinism, understanding research is important across a wide variety of disciplines. The importance of research and statistics is crucial to most disciplines in a university. Obviously the physical sciences, social sciences, and even certain areas of the fine arts are grounded in research. Business, engineering, and many applied disciplines depend on basic and applied research for understanding and the use of knowledge in each discipline.

As a citizen or in a career, an educated person knowledgeable about research is able to make wise decisions, rather than just being told what to do by other people. An educated person learns about logic, research, and statistics, and applies the knowledge and understanding to make wise decisions whenever and wherever appropriate.

Chapter 8

An Attitude

"Wise men lay up knowledge, but the babbling
of a fool brings ruin near"

(Prov. 10:14).

I hope the discussions of context, free will/determinism, and decision-making have piqued your curiosity about knowledge and understanding. It is worth noting that these are just three of many ideas I could have chosen. I could have developed the role of policies on political matters and what they have meant to history, as well as their economic, social, and psychological implications; or I could have developed the importance of logic in critical thinking. Understanding these and many more ideas will help you to become more knowledgeable, and to gain deeper understanding and hopefully more wisdom.

A decision to be a Proverbial student will be reflected in your curiosity about knowledge and understanding. Your attitude about school will be to pursue an education and all that entails.

In all of my classes, I tried to help all students understand that you cannot gain knowledge without good study habits. Since one of my areas of interest is memory, I always pointed out to students that research has clearly demonstrated that new abstract information that is not rehearsed is usually lost within thirty to sixty seconds. You need to take good notes and frequently review the information. You need to manipulate the information, make it concrete, make it personal, and relate it to known information to make learning easier. You cannot do that by sitting and waiting to be entertained.

My weaker students usually made one or more of the following four big mistakes. First, they did not attend class. Second, they did not take good notes. Third, they tried to read and memorize details rather than gain knowledge. Fourth, they had the wrong priority for work and play.

Attend class. With the obvious exception of online classes, class attendance is crucial to success. I have found that many bright Christians often were allowed to miss classes in high school for various activities. Since they were good Christian students, their teachers understood their situations, and class work was easy to make up. College professors are not usually as understanding, and you need to hear the lectures to make good grades.

Our youngest son went to Georgia Tech as an undergraduate. He found and followed the party life his freshman year. When he brought his grades home, we discussed the military as a place where he could grow up—and which would not cost as much money. He returned to school and finished with considerable success.

Later, he attended graduate school at Duke. His first-year grades put him near the top of his class in one of the best graduate programs in the nation. I knew he was capable of excellent schoolwork and was not surprised by his success. I asked him, "What is the difference between your bad performance your freshman year and your excellent performance in graduate school?" He told me two things: "Dad, good grades are easy if you go to class." And, "Dad, you paid for Georgia Tech; I am paying for Duke, so I never missed a class."

Even the best of Christians find excuses to not go to class. They convince themselves that the Lord wants them to go on a mission activity, or they are up all night counseling a friend. You need to be in the presence of the knowledge to gain the knowledge. In other words: Attend class.

Take good notes. In high school, very bright students were often able to just listen in class and perform better on exams than lesser students. They did not have to take good notes and study. Unfortunately, as a result, they are frequently overwhelmed by college. Even though they are bright, they do not have the habits for academic success. You must know how to take good notes. Organize your notes into the most important points, with the details subordinate to those points. Take a few minutes after every class and review your notes, to be sure they will make sense in a couple of weeks—before an exam.

Gain knowledge. Students often try too hard to memorize details. They get out their highlighters, and get bogged down. The details faced in college are too numerous to memorize. As discussed in the chapter on context, learn to listen and read for the big picture. Memorizing thousands of individual details is gaining facts, not necessarily gaining knowledge that will lead to understanding.

Priorities. Down time and play are important. Christ often took time apart from his work to pray and be refreshed. The issue is not whether to play or not; the issue is *when* to play. Proverbial students get work done and *then* play. They make an enjoyable activity the reward for work accomplished. Weaker students play, and then try to squeeze in their work.

If you are on an intramural team and want to participate in a big game, get your homework done before the game. Proper prioritizing accomplishes two things: You get more work done, and you enjoy your play time because you are not worrying about the work you need to do after the game.

I hope that being a Proverbial student will be the academic attitude of all Christian students, not those in a particular curriculum. I hope it is an attitude you will carry into all classes, carry into all majors, and continue throughout life. Most universities, during the first two years of study, require students to meet general education requirements. Liberal arts universities and degree programs expand that education into all four years of undergraduate study. Students in most professional programs go into applied courses for their junior and senior years. Thus, business and nursing students will take similar courses the first two years, and then enter applied courses appropriate to their disciplines for the last two years.

In my experience at regional universities, many students who intend to major in professional areas such as business or engineering view the first two years as unnecessary electives or "the basics." They cannot wait to get through them and into their "real" courses. They view the basic courses as hurdles to be cleared so they can get into courses that will get them a job. They fail to see the basic courses as the knowledge that will make them educated people. They want degrees, they want jobs. I would like to see that attitude remolded in Christian students.

All courses should be approached with a curiosity about ideas, and with a desire for knowledge, understanding, and wisdom. Christian businessmen and women, doctors, nurses, engineers, teachers, and other professionals need to know about the arts, political science, communication, psychology, sociology, history, other countries, other languages, philosophy, the sciences, and mathematics in order to positively influence our culture.

Equally important, professional courses should be approached with the attitude of a Proverbial student. Professional students who get grades and earn degrees, but do not gain knowledge and understanding in their professional courses, will have a difficult time getting jobs—and have an even more difficult time keeping them, in our ever-changing world.

As mentioned earlier, our oldest son's best friend in high school received his education at a public university in the South. He got an excellent engineering degree. His first job, and the one he held until his death, was at a major defense facility. He was very successful.

However, one of the major keys to his success was not his engineering education, although that was important. He was also able to use the knowledge he gained as a Proverbial student in discussions during coffee breaks, which proved to be very important. By showing curiosity, knowledge, understanding, and wisdom in a wide variety of subjects, he gained the trust of colleagues and his superiors. That trust led to a very productive work environment and excellent personal satisfaction.

He had a good education; he was a lifelong learner; he was a devoted Christian; he met my definition of a Proverbial student. His knowledge, understanding, and wisdom beyond his professional knowledge served him very well in a highly competitive field. His applied education was good, but not sufficient for success.

My concern is for knowledge, understanding, and wisdom to be important for every Christian student. I hope you chose to adopt the attitude and approach of a Proverbial student, I pray that your study habits lead to success in school, and that the knowledge and understanding you attain lead to success in your chosen field.

Chapter 9
Spiritual Wisdom and Academic Wisdom

"Avoid the Godless mixture of contradictory notions
which is falsely known as 'knowledge'—some have
followed and have lost their faith"

(1 Tim. 6:20–21, PHILLIPS).

Throughout this book, I have tried to convince you to pursue knowledge, understanding, and wisdom as university students. I need to be very clear: In no way am I suggesting that academic knowledge should *replace* spiritual knowledge and wisdom. Academic knowledge should *enhance* spiritual knowledge and wisdom.

The writers of Proverbs had spiritual wisdom for their primary focus—the wisdom that comes from knowing God through Bible study, worship, fellowship, meditation, prayer, and other disciplines. I certainly want you to develop and continue spiritual growth through those activities.

On campus, students will come into contact with academic knowledge that challenges Christian beliefs. The Bible offers several warnings about false knowledge. A clear warning was from Paul to Timothy: "Timothy, guard most carefully your divine commission. Avoid the Godless mixture of contradictory notions which is falsely known as 'knowledge'—some have followed and have lost their faith" (1 Tim. 6:20, PHILLIPS).

Some people would interpret this passage as a warning against all academic knowledge. I had numerous students who were warned by parents and preachers to be leery of university professors and their false teachings.

Paul's warning is a good warning—false knowledge can be misleading! But clearly, two things should be noted: First, false knowledge can arise within the church, as well on a college campus. The rise of false wisdom and teaching within the church may be more devastating to your faith than knowledge encountered while attending a university. Most of the warnings about false teachings found in the New Testament are about teaching that can or has arisen within a religious setting, not an academic one.

Second, a warning about false knowledge is not an excuse to fail to seek academic knowledge. Paul is not saying avoid knowledge; he is saying avoid the contradictions of *false* knowledge.

A good academic education will give you tools to make decisions about false knowledge, as well as knowledge that enables you to interpret ideas, provides ways to think, and ways to solve problems. All of these tools are valuable and are helpful for making wise decisions. Such educational knowledge will strengthen, not weaken, your faith—if you correctly learn and use it.

The Internet provides many good examples of how an academic education can enhance wisdom and avoid false ideas. Time and time again, students came to me with ideas they had heard from a trusted friend on the Internet. Weak students do not have the tools to decide for themselves about the truth or falsehood of the information. Students with a good education have the statistical, logical, evidential, and other tools necessary to support or reject the information.

Whether it is global warming, medical care, capital punishment, or a variety of very important, very complex ideas, many students accept ideas that are passed on to them simply because they trust the messenger. They do not think for themselves.

Often students would come to my office and ask important relevant questions such as "Do you believe in global warming?" I have my personal ideas about global warming, and other social issues. However, most of the time I did not share personal preference; I usually asked students questions to challenge them, to see if they were thinking about the topic. I wanted them to learn to decide what is false knowledge.

In the case of global warming, I typically replied with questions such as: "I have visited Alaska and New Zealand in recent years. The vast majority of the glaciers are receding. Is that evidence for or against global warming?" I also showed them a *National Geographic* map of the far north of the Northern Hemisphere, which shows the snow and ice caps a few years ago compared to their current formations. I ask, "The snow and ice caps are clearly smaller today than they were just a few years ago. Is that evidence for or against global warming?"

I have presented this evidence many times, and the typical response was along the lines of "I can tell that you are one of those Al Gore tree-huggers." Other students jumped to the conclusion that I was in favor of reduced emissions, certain treaties, or a variety of assumed causes and solutions to global warming.

The responses demonstrated the students were not good listeners. I never said I believed in global warming; I only asked them whether or not the evidence I presented was for or against global warming. My questions were not statements of my personal position, but a way to get them to examine their own positions.

All too often, this was as far as the conversation went. They left my office clinging to the position they had when they entered; they did not want evidence to interfere with what they believed. I wanted them to have an examined position of their own, and they rejected the process of examining their positions.

Psychologists have shown that our fundamental tendencies are to adopt a position, and then look for evidence in support of our positions. When confronted with evidence against a position, we tend to ignore it, find fault with it, or strengthen our commitment to our position. We do not want to weigh the evidence and decide whether knowledge is true or false.

The tendency is in full view during any political campaign. People decide to support one candidate for whatever reason. Once they have made that commitment, they only accept or believe positive information about their candidate. If counterevidence arises, it is ignored. People just yell louder for their candidate and find more outrageous claims to make against their opponent.

Wise people learn to examine a variety of positions, see the plusses and minuses for the positions, and decide what is true or what is false because of evidence and logic. Lacking evidence, you may need to take leaps of faith, but do so knowingly.

Clear-thinking people keep important questions and issues separate; muddled thinkers jump from one issue to another, seeking support for their entrenched position.

Christian students are human. You have adopted many positions because of your parents, teacher, peers, or pastors.

You have the tendency to disregard negative evidence and search for evidence to support your views. You need knowledge, understanding, and wisdom to critically examine your positions on social, political, and faith issues, and then decide if knowledge is true or false. Many Christian students are afraid to carefully examine a position that comes from a parent or a pastor because such an examination might seem like it is challenging authority and possibly their faith. I believe you should carefully examine and develop your own positions. In my experience, examining my political, social, cultural, or other beliefs in the light of the Bible and academic knowledge has strengthened my faith.

You do not need to be a Republican because your parents are Republicans, any more than you need to be a Democrat because your parents are Republicans. You need to make your own choices based on knowledge, sound logic, and understanding.

I do not want students to blindly accept or reject parents or pastors. I do not want students to blindly adopt my personal positions. I want you to thoughtfully examine and adopt your own positions.

You must work hard to be good listeners, to not focus on the exception, and to overcome the strong tendency to ignore negative evidence. You need to examine a variety of positions— to see the strengths and weaknesses of your own positions as well as opposing positions. Whenever possible, you should develop understanding and make wise decisions from evidence. Lacking evidence, you may take leaps of faith, but you do so knowingly.

The Bible imparts knowledge. A college education will increase your knowledge and help understanding and wisdom. Throughout your life, I encourage you to seek knowledge, understanding, and wisdom in all areas of life. Read good books and discuss them with others; watch television shows and movies that expand your knowledge and understanding; use the Internet as a resource, and not just as a source of entertainment.

We need Christian students who are sound thinkers. We need Christian students who understand evidence, logic, and decision-making and who have the knowledge from many disciplines to make wise decisions in our needy world. A good academic education will enhance your faith walk. Pursue an education! Be a Proverbial student!

Chapter 10

Graduation and Commencement

"Listen to advice and accept instruction, that you
may gain wisdom for the future"

(Prov. 19:20).

Students who cross the stage to get a diploma hopefully have
gained knowledge to make a degree meaningful. I hope anyone
who has that privilege will pay attention to the two names used
to identify the event. On the one hand, the event is a *graduation*
from college—a sign of work accomplished. On the other hand,
the event is a *commencement*—a sign of a life to be lived. Each
word frames a context for the event, and both contexts are
important.

I am confident that most students and parents are aware of
the first context. The money spent, the many hours of lectures,
the many tests taken, the papers written, and the books read, all
add up to a major work effort. Graduation is a proper time for
you to celebrate work accomplished.

My concern is that few students and parents recognize and
accept the joy of the second context. Most are not commencing
a lifetime of learning—they are seeking a job. They see college as
an end, and not as a means that enables learning throughout life.

College should provide a knowledge foundation. A Proverbial student graduates and uses that knowledge to commence a lifelong learning experience. Lifelong curiosity is the real key to being an educated person. To highlight this idea, I want to make a strong statement: College is not a necessary condition for a person to be a Proverbial student.

My mother lived to be in her nineties. She lived in western Kansas during the Great Depression with a single-parent mother; she could not afford to go to college. However, she adopted the attitude of a Proverbial student. She remained curious about knowledge throughout her life. She was an avid reader, a student of politics, of geography, of history, and of matters of faith. She would have more knowledge if she had attended college; but she had more knowledge, understanding, and wisdom about her world than many people with higher degrees. She was a highly educated woman with a high school degree.

I hope you get degrees and celebrate hard work accomplished. My deeper hope is that at some point in time you become Proverbial students and enjoy gaining knowledge throughout your lives. I hope you achieve understanding and, with God's grace, become wise people. Let's close by looking at what this could look like in your life.

Chapter 11

A Lifelong Proverbial Student

"Happy is the man who finds wisdom, and the man who gains understanding, for the gain from it is better than the gain from silver and its profit better than gold"

(Prov. 3:13–14).

Being a Proverbial student during college will greatly increase your knowledge base, but Proverbial students will continue to learn and grow throughout their lives. Wisdom may increase with age and experience, but knowledge, understanding, and wisdom should be sought at every age.

As previously stated, my growth into being a Proverbial student has actually been greater since I graduated from college. I have continued to gain knowledge. One interesting development is: The more I learn, the more I realize I do not know. God has created an enormous and complicated world. I will never have all knowledge, but the joy of gaining new knowledge is a joy I hope to continue until the Lord calls me home.

Stewardship

As I have gained knowledge and matured in understanding, I have gained wisdom in my faith walk. A clear example of my growth is my understanding of the idea of stewardship.

Throughout the majority of our lives, my wife and I taught Sunday school classes for college students. When we were young, we decided to gain knowledge in one of our classes and try to understand what the Bible said about money. The students did not have a lot of money, nor did we, but we wanted to gain knowledge and understanding while we were without money. If and when we earned more than just enough to make ends meet, we wanted to be wise with our decisions.

We decided to read the Bible from Genesis to Revelation. Class members volunteered to read one section each and report on it. Each person read a section and then wrote down any verses they thought applied to money. They brought those verses to the class and we discussed them.

Some books had many applications; some had none. As we worked our way through the Old and then New Testaments, I came to realize that I lacked great knowledge and understanding about a critical idea in the Christian faith—stewardship.

The cornerstone idea for good stewardship is to believe that all we have comes from God. I did not have that knowledge and understanding. I naively assumed I earned my money; as long as I tithed I did not have to feel guilty about how I spent the rest.

What became abundantly clear to me was tithing, though important, was a secondary idea. The idea that is discussed and practiced the most is the concept of first fruits. We are told to give the first and the best to the full-time church. In former times, the first would have been the results of the harvest. Today it is more likely to be the results of a paycheck.

I believe the reason first fruits are so important is the acknowledgement that all comes from God. By giving the first and best, I acknowledge that all comes from God and that I am responsible for all of my time, talent, and resources. He has invested in me, and I am to be responsible for the entire investment. My decisions about all of my purchases are just as important as my tithe to the church.

Unfortunately, the word "stewardship" often conjures up images of old people asking for money in church. Good stewardship means that we are responsible for good stewardship throughout our lives, with *everything* in our lives.

Most students and young graduates do not have a lot of money, so stewardship is not an important idea for them. Even worse, when they have a little money, they believe it is their money. They might believe that ten percent is God's but that the rest is theirs. They do not understand that all is from God: time and talent as well as money.

We are called to be good stewards over all of our time, talents, and money—*all* of our resources. We are to have the knowledge to be wise in all of our purchases and the use of our time and talents.

To try to help put stewardship over all resources during college in proper perspective, consider the following questions:

Will a particular head cover make someone a better Christian?

Will any hairstyle make someone a better Christian?

Will a tattoo make someone a better Christian?

Will any personal adornment make someone a better Christian?

Will any clothing make someone a better Christian?

Will any vehicle make someone a better Christian?

The answer, in each and every case, is *no*!

In Matthew 6:19–21 (PHILLIPS) we are told: "Don't pile up treasures on earth, where moth and rust can spoil them and thieves can break in and steal. But keep your treasure in heaven where there is neither moth nor rust to spoil it and nobody can break in and steal. For wherever your treasure is, there is your heart too!"

Please note carefully, I am not saying a Christian should not have a tattoo, fine clothes, or a new car. In the light of the scripture from Matthew, the question to contemplate is "What should my treasure *be?*"

I believe wisdom is a heavenly treasure to be sought before earthly material goods. Whatever is put into a mind, heart, and soul can be a treasure to cherish. Certainly spiritual activities will help us to become wiser persons by guiding what goes into our hearts. Beyond the spiritual experiences of fellowship, worship, Bible study, meditation, and other meaningful activities, becoming a Proverbial person is helped by being a good steward over the experiences that give knowledge and understanding: the books read, the lectures listened to, the discussions carried on, the appropriate Internet sites watched, the informative TV and movies watched, as well as other information-gathering experiences.

If knowledge is gained, if knowledge is processed for understanding, and if knowledge and understanding are used to help make decisions, then we will become wiser people. Clearly Proverbial students who are good stewards over all of their time, talents, and resources will be wiser and better people. Knowledge, understanding, and wisdom should enable people to love the Lord God with all of their hearts, minds, souls, and strength; enable them to love others; and enable them to appropriately love themselves.

Ask yourself the following question: Do I put more time and energy into the pursuit of knowledge and understanding to make me a wiser and better person, or do I spend more time in pursuit of material goods that are stored up on earth and therefore subject to rot, rust, and theft? Where is my treasure?

God wants us to be stewards over our resources: our time, our talents, and our money. We are responsible for every decision because all we have comes from him. I suggest that good stewards spend a major portion of their time, especially in college, in the pursuit of knowledge, understanding, and wisdom. A Proverbial student is a good steward.

Dialogue

A second of many areas about which I have gained knowledge, understanding, and hopefully some wisdom is the process called dialogue. A wise person engages in dia*logue*, not dia*tribe*. A good dialogue requires the interested parties to commit to listening to each other, to being willing to acknowledge the strengths in the position of the other side, and to being willing to admit the weaknesses in their own positions. Then and only then have the parties earned the right to criticize each other. That takes courage.

I have found dialogue missing in many aspects of modern life. Very few people—whether on television, the print media, the Internet, or the living room—engage in genuine dialogue about race, politics, religion, sports, personal relationships, or a host of other topics. Most people simply want to make self-righteous claims for their own positions and mawkish putdowns of the other side.

Several factors contribute to this lack of dialogue in America. The first is human nature. As stated previously, psychologists have known for years that most people form an opinion and then look for information that supports their position. When confronted with facts contrary to a position, people just yell louder or find more outrageous claims to make against their opponents.

In addition to the frailties of human cognitive processing, an important reason for the lack of dialogue is many people in the public eye are educated in debate, public relations, persuasion, or the American judicial system. They are not educated to listen; they are trained to make vigorous defenses of their established opinions, or vigorous attacks on other positions. They deny or ignore strengths in other positions and weaknesses in their own positions. Winning a debate, spinning a position, covering for losses, winning a trial, or winning an election are all more important than understanding and truth. As a result, the average person observes and participates in many more well-spun diatribes than dialogues.

When conflicts occur, most people are unwilling to see the positives in others, or to examine the problems in their own positions. We seek evidence in support of our positions and choose to ignore clear evidence that does not support our position. Thus, when conflicting positions occur, we prefer to race straight into a diatribe, finding fault with the other side.

The certainty of many Christians makes dialogue difficult even within the church. Certainty leads to diatribe and not dialogue and wisdom. All too often, we have our positions, we are right, and no one is going to convince us differently. The role of the church in the lives of Galileo and Copernicus was not just ancient history; we see it acted out in many modern-day issues.

Christ tried to warn us with His wise question in Matthew 7:3 (PHILLIPS): "Why do you look at the speck of sawdust in your brother's eye and fail to notice the plank in your own?" We need more people who are willing to look at their own planks before they attack other positions. We need Proverbial students who understand and are willing to practice dialogue in order to make progress in race relations, political understanding, church unity, and many more areas. We need you to seek solutions, develop understanding, and engage in genuine dialogues.

The lack of dialogue in our political system and our daily lives is an enormous problem. We desperately need Proverbial students to be educated and practicing dialogue. We need you to influence our policy debates, before our country is reduced to simply "the loudest side wins." We need you to practice dialogue within your home to build better marriages and families.

* * *

I have many more lessons I could share. My hope and prayer is that you become a Proverbial student and pursue knowledge, develop understanding, and gain wisdom in your own life lessons.

The proverb at the beginning of this chapter is a good one for lifelong Proverbial students: "Happy is the man who finds wisdom, and the man who gains understanding, for the gain from it is better than the gain from silver and its profit better than gold" (Prov. 3:13–14). A life of wisdom is far better than a life of wealth and diatribe. My prayer for Christian students, is that you become Proverbial students—enjoying a life of wisdom and using knowledge, understanding, and wisdom to make a difference in our very needy world.

Appendix

List of Proverbs

Chapter 1: "An intelligent mind acquires knowledge, and the ear of the wise seeks knowledge" (Prov. 18:15).

Chapter 2: "A degree may be something to fall back on, but an education will lift you up" (personal proverb).

Chapter 3: "The fear of the Lord is the beginning of knowledge; fools despise wisdom and instruction" (Prov. 1:7).

Chapter 4: "The wise man also may hear and increase in learning, and the man of understanding acquire skill, to understand a proverb and a figure, the words of the wise and their riddles" (Prov. 1:5–6).

Chapter 5: "It is not good for a man to be without knowledge" (Prov. 19:2).

Chapter 6: "Free will is important, but an informed will makes wise decisions" (personal proverb).

Chapter 7: "Wisdom abides in the mind of a man of understanding, but it is not known in the heart of fools" (Prov. 14:33).

Chapter 8: "Wise men lay up knowledge, but the babbling of a fool brings ruin near" (Prov. 10:14).

Chapter 9: "Avoid the Godless mixture of contradictory notions which is falsely known as 'knowledge'—some have followed and have lost their faith" (1 Tim. 6:20, PHILLIPS).

Chapter 10: "Listen to advice and accept instruction, that you may gain wisdom for the future" (Prov. 19:20).

Chapter 11: "Happy is the man who finds wisdom, and the man who gains understanding, for the gain from it is better than the gain from silver and its profit better than gold" (Prov. 3:13–14).

Endnotes

1. J. D. Bransford and M. K. Johnson, "Some Investigations of Comprehension and Recall," *Journal of Verbal Learning and Verbal Behavior* 11, (1972): 717–726.

2. Sue Grafton, *U is for Undertow* (New York: G. P. Putnam's Sons, 2009), 1.

3. Tony Hillerman, *Dance Hall of the Dead* (New York: Harper & Row, 1973), 77.